# THE BIG BOOK OF SECRETS

YF IOU YTNA WOTE B AYP SNEH
TSIH TS IEH TKOO BRO FUO

If you need help
deciphering this
code, the answer
is on Page 2.

3 bcd

Other books by GYLES BRANDRETH

THE DAFT DICTIONARY
JOKES, JOKES, JOKES: A JOKE FOR EVERY DAY OF THE YEAR
CHALLENGE
CRAZY DAYS
THE CRAZY ENCYCLOPAEDIA
THE CRAZY WORD BOOK
THE BIG BOOK OF MAGIC
THE BIG BOOK OF OPTICAL ILLUSIONS
SHADOW SHOWS
THE CRAZY BOOK OF WORLD RECORDS
1000 RIDDLES: THE GREATEST BOOK OF RIDDLES EVER
1000 JOKES: THE GREATEST JOKE BOOK EVER KNOWN
1000 QUESTIONS: THE GREATEST QUIZ BOOK
1000 FACTS: THE GREATEST BOOK OF AMAZING INFORMATION

All published by CAROUSEL BOOKS

**The secret message is**
IF YOU WANT TO BE A SPY THEN THIS
IS THE BOOK FOR YOU

# THE BIG BOOK OF SECRETS
A CAROUSEL BOOK 0 552 54123 0

First publication in Great Britain
PRINTING HISTORY
Carousel edition published 1977
Carousel edition reprinted 1978
Carousel edition reprinted 1978
Carousel edition reprinted 1979
Carousel edition reprinted 1982
Copyright © Gyles Brandreth 1977
Illustrator's copyright © Transworld Publishers Ltd. 1977

This book is set in Monotype Garamond

Carousel Books are published by
Transworld Publishers Ltd.
Century House, 61–63 Uxbridge Road,
Ealing, London W5 5SA

Set, printed and bound in Great Britain by
Cox & Wyman Ltd, Reading

Gyles Brandreth

# THE BIG BOOK OF SECRETS

illustrated by LOUIS HELLMAN

**CAROUSEL**
A DIVISION OF TRANSWORLD PUBLISHERS LTD

## CONTENTS

| | Page |
|---|---|
| Introduction | 8 |
| Who's Who In The Spy Ring | 9 |
| Hiding Your Equipment | 13 |
| Carrying Secret Messages | 16 |
| Drops and Pick-ups | 22 |
| You'd Better Go In Disguise | 33 |
| Secret Writing | 45 |
| Codes and Ciphers | 52 |
| Sign Language | 119 |

**THIS BOOK BELONGS TO:** ....................
             (Real name to be written in invisible ink)

**CODE NAME:**              ....................

**ADDRESS:**                ....................

                            ....................

**TELEPHONE NUMBER:**       ....................

**PHOTOGRAPH**  
(Stick a photograph of yourself in heavy disguise here.)

**FINGERPRINT**  
(Don't worry: it's a false fingerprint.)

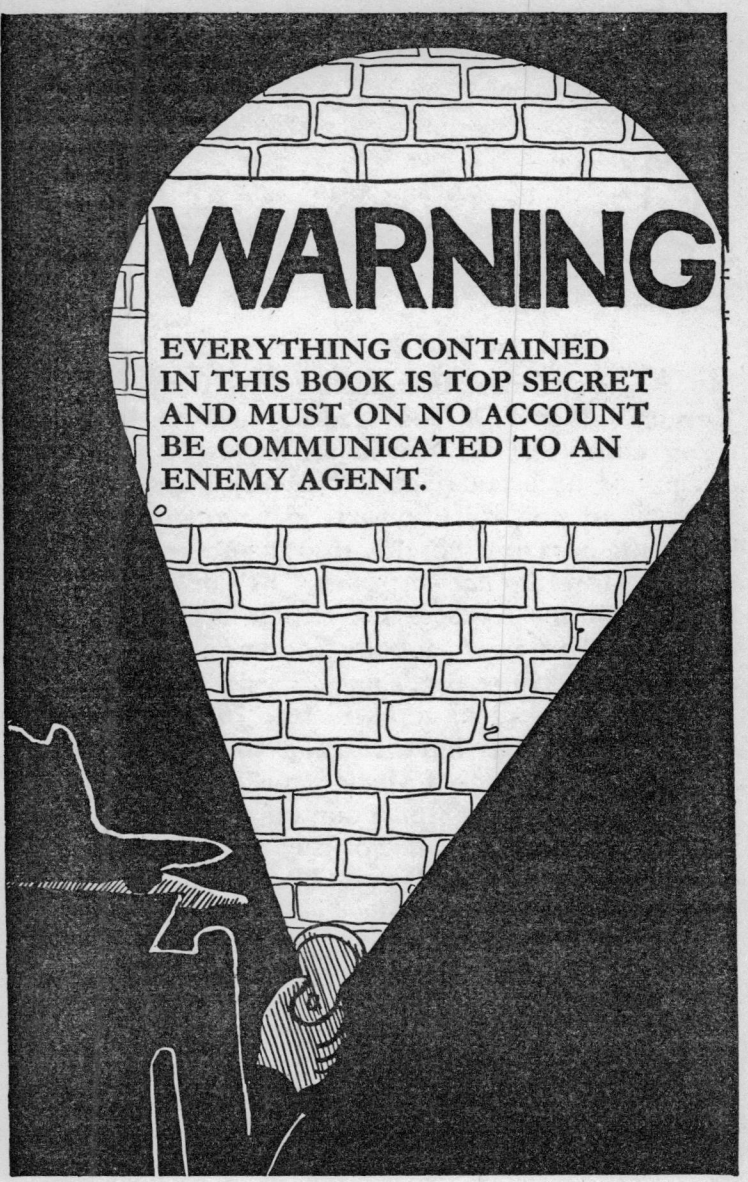

# INTRODUCTION

My name's Gyles Brandreth. Or Harry Nix. Or Jimmy Goldoni. Or Tom Tiddletumdum. Or something completely different. In my time, I've used dozens of different names. Nobody knows my *real* name. And nobody knows who I work for. Spying is my business, but whether my masters are America's Central Intelligence Agency, Britain's MI5, the Soviet Union's KGB or the Secret Service of some other foreign power, nobody knows and nobody will ever know because that's one secret I intend to keep. All my other secrets you will find in the pages that follow. When you have learned them you will be equipped to become a Master Spy. Who knows, but one day you might find yourself working for me? Or I might find myself working for you. When we do meet, feel free to call me X. Until then, I'm signing myself, yours anonymously,

*Gyles Brandreth*

# WHO'S WHO IN THE SPY RING

## THE MASTER SPY

He is in command of the Spy Ring. Very few people ever meet him and no one knows his real name.

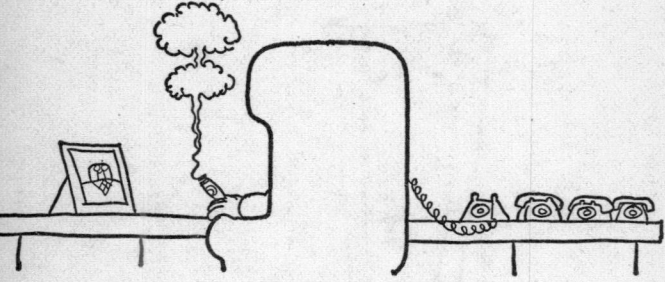

## THE COURIERS

They are the secret agents who take the messages and orders from the Master Spy to the other spies and take the spies' reports back to the Master Spy.

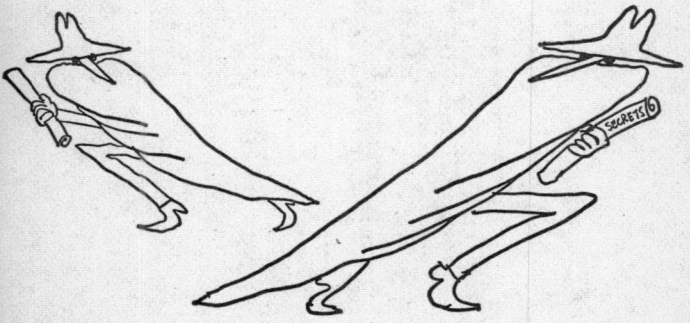

# THE SPIES

### THE SECRET AGENT
who works for the Master Spy

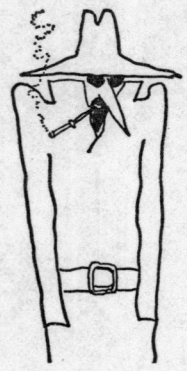

### THE DOUBLE AGENT
who works for two Master Spies and is double-crossing them

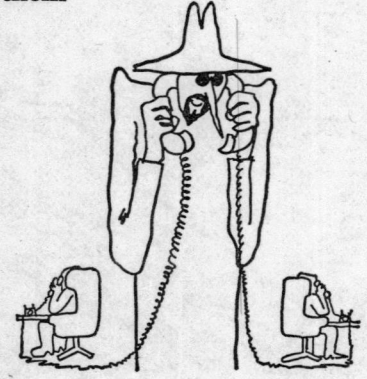

## THE CONTACT
The spy who meets other spies and passes on information

## THE SHADOW
The spy who follows enemy agents and keeps an eye on on their movements

# HIDE and SEEK

# HIDING YOUR EQUIPMENT

You would never guess to look at this room that it contained a mass of secret agent's equipment – but it does. Hidden in the room are a two-way radio for sending secret messages, a spy's tape recorder, invisible inks, special disguises, secret maps and code books. If you turn over the page you will be able to look at the room with X-ray eyes and see exactly where the equipment has been hidden.

What where? One map is stuck under the chair. The code books are under a floor-board, The invisible inks are in the jug and the vase. The beard and spectacles, the maps and secret documents are behind the pictures, the tape recorder is under the mattress at the foot of the bed, and the two-way radio is under the pillow.

You should always keep the *Big Book of Secrets* well hidden. If you can find a very big, old book that nobody wants and nobody will mind if you cut up, you can open it and cut out a hole in the middle to make it into a secret box:

Another good idea is to take a big box and mark it **SECRET**. Inside the **SECRET** box put anything you like that *isn't* really secret! Keep your real secrets in a different box that isn't marked. If the enemy raid your room they will take away the box marked **SECRET** and will leave the real box of secrets behind!

# CARRYING SECRET MESSAGES

Carrying secret messages is always dangerous. No one must know you are carrying them. And if you get caught, whatever happens, the message must not be found.

This spy is carrying seventeen secret messages. Can you guess where he is hiding them?

1. **INSIDE THE HAT BAND ON THE OUTSIDE**

2. **ON YOUR HEAD, UNDER YOUR HAT**

3. **TUCKED INSIDE THE HAT BAND INSIDE YOUR HAT**

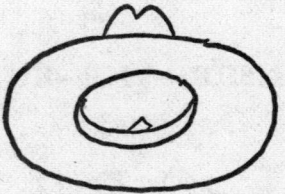

4. **PINNED TO THE INSIDE OF YOUR HAT**

## 5. PINNED BEHIND THE LAPEL OF YOUR COAT OR JACKET OR BLAZER

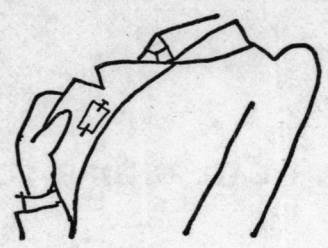

## 6. TUCKED INSIDE THE BACK OF YOUR SHIRT OR BLOUSE COLLAR

## 7. TUCKED INSIDE THE KNOT OF YOUR TIE

## 8. PINNED ON TO THE BACK OF YOUR TIE

## 9. INSIDE YOUR BALL-POINT PEN

## 10. INSIDE THE CUFFS OF YOUR COAT

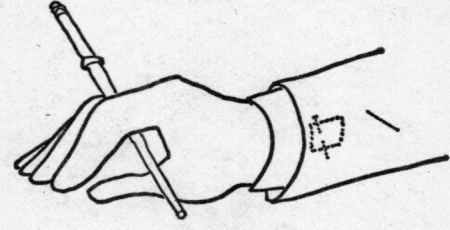

## 11. TUCKED INSIDE YOUR WATCH STRAP

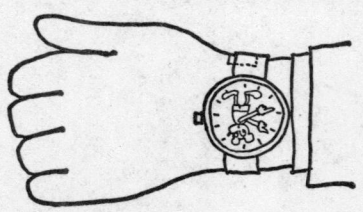

12. **PINNED ON THE INSIDE OF YOUR BELT**

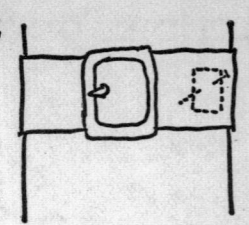

13. **PINNED ON THE HIDDEN SIDE OF THE HEM OF YOUR SKIRT OR KILT**

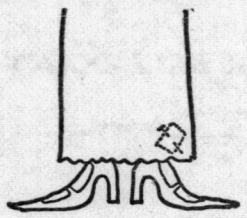

14. **TUCKED INTO THE TURN-UPS ON YOUR TROUSERS**

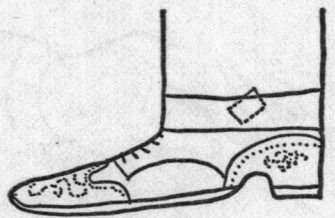

15. **HIDDEN UNDER THE PLASTER COVERING THE 'GRAZE' ON YOUR KNEE**

## 16. INSIDE YOUR SOCKS

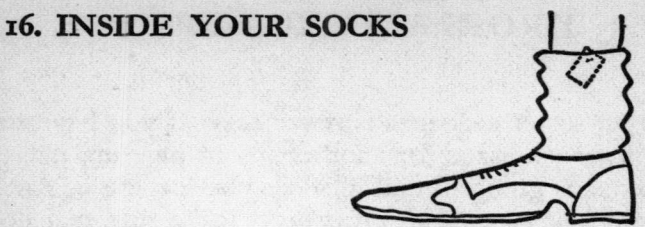

## 17. UNDER THE FALSE SOLE OF YOUR SHOE

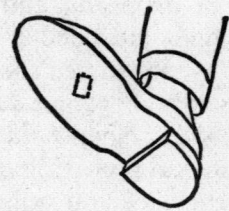

To make a false sole for your shoe, put the shoe on to a piece of thick paper or thin card, draw round it and cut out the shape:

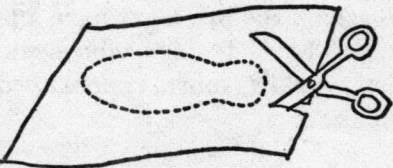

Now put the false sole inside your shoe, with the message hidden under it:

# DROPS AND PICK-UPS

Delivering secret messages is never easy. If you have to leave a secret message for another spy to pick up, make sure no one is going to find it or see you leaving it. And if you are sent to pick up a message, make sure that no one spots you. A hiding-place for secret messages is called a 'drop' or a 'dead-letter box'.

Here are ten different scenes that will show you ten different ways of dropping and picking up secret messages. All of them are used by professional spies and secret agents. Try not to use the same method too often, or the enemy may start to get suspicious. After all, there may be somebody 'shadowing' you, following you wherever you go and reporting on your every movement. If there is and they see you going to meet the same man on the same park bench every Tuesday afternoon at 4.00 p.m., they might begin to suspect that the man you meet is your contact and that he is passing you secret information at your weekly meetings – and they might be right!

In these ten scenes the messages have all been dropped by a courier called Max. The spy who is picking them up is one of the world's most experienced and daring agents: code-name Zip.

# SCENE 1

MAX is taking his dog for a walk. The secret message is tucked under the dog's collar. As they wander through the park they pass a bench on which ZIP is sitting. He leans forward to scratch the dog's head, and as he does so removes the secret message from under the dog's collar. Max walks on. Neither of them has exchanged a word, but Zip now has the secret message in his hand!

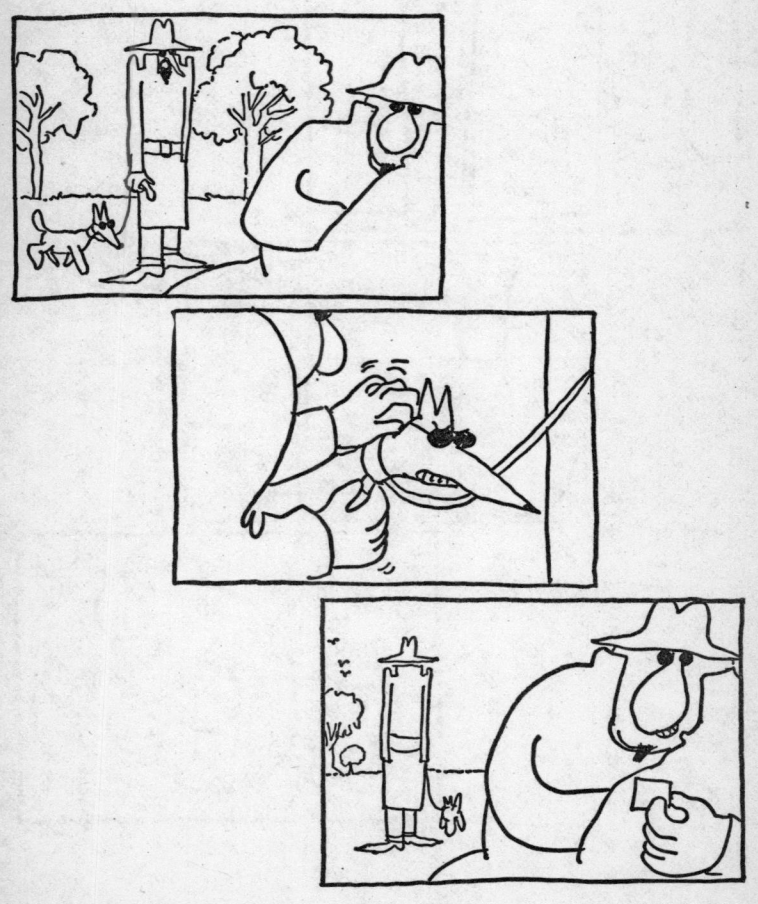

# SCENE 2

MAX is dressed up as a man who sells newspapers on the street corner. ZIP comes along and buys a newspaper. The secret message is tucked inside the newspaper.

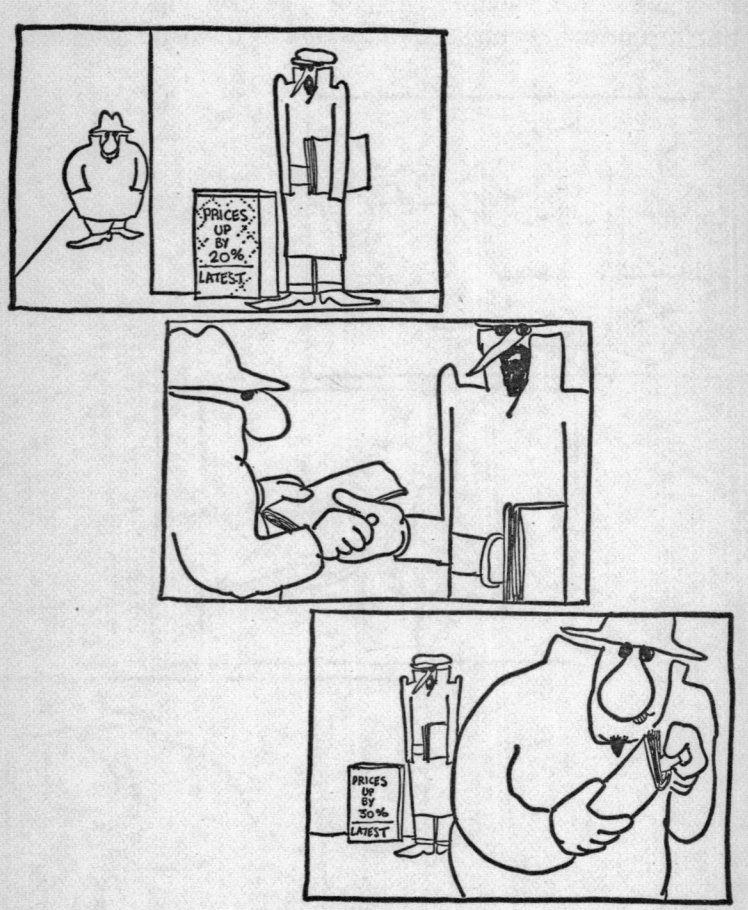

# SCENE 3

MAX wraps the secret message in a small plastic envelope and buries the envelope in a flower-bed or window-box. ZIP comes along later and pretends to smell the beautiful flowers. As he sniffs at them he digs into the soil with his hand and unearths the secret message.

# SCENE 4

MAX folds the message into as small a size as he can and then tucks it into a crack in the wall. If you look at any brick wall, you will see lots of little gaps where the cement has come out: the gaps are tiny, but they are still big enough to be used as 'dead-letter boxes'. ZIP comes along later and removes the message from the crack in the wall.

# SCENE 5

MAX hides the secret message on the ground under a stone. ZIP later comes along and stubs his toe on the stone. He bends down to rub his sore toe and removes the secret message from underneath the stone.

# SCENE 6

MAX and ZIP are both seen hurrying along a busy street carrying black umbrellas. Max is coming from one direction. Zip is coming from the opposite direction. They are obviously both in a tremendous rush, so much so that they bump into each other and knock each other over! They pick themselves up, apologise to each other, pick up their umbrellas and walk on. The clever part of the operation is this: when they got up, Max picked up Zip's umbrella and Zip picked up Max's umbrella. The secret message was hidden inside Max's umbrella.

# SCENE 7

MAX visits the local golf course and hides the secret message in one of the holes. Later in the day, ZIP plays a round of golf and when he gets his ball into the hole, he goes to pick out the ball and removes the secret message at the same time. (The same method can be used with other holes: for example, you can leave the message in a rabbit hole and pick it up while pretending to look for rabbits.)

# SCENE 8

MAX pins the secret message underneath a wooden bench in the park or under a deck-chair on the beach. ZIP comes along later and sits on the bench or the deck-chair and removes the secret message.

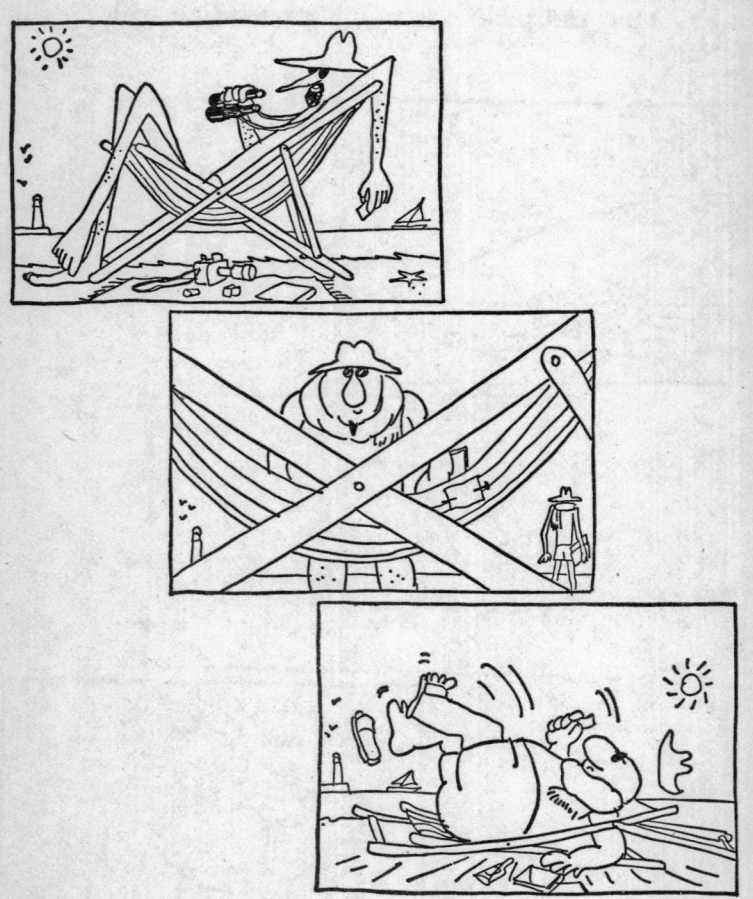

# SCENE 9

MAX is working in the local library. ZIP comes to take out a library book. Zip takes the book to Max for Max to check. As he checks it he slips the secret message inbetween the pages of the book. He gives the book to Zip who leaves the library with the book and the secret message.

# SCENE 10

MAX folds up the secret message and hides it inside in empty matchbox or cigarette pack. He then drops the matchbox or pack in the street. ZIP comes along and stops by the dropped box or pack and bends down to tie up his shoe lace. As he ties the shoe lace, he picks up the matchbox or cigarette pack that contains the secret message.

# YOU'D BETTER GO IN DISGUISE

If you go out to deliver a secret message today, you'd better go in disguise. The best disguises for spies and secret agents are ones that can be put on quickly and taken off even more quickly. You want to go into your house looking like this:

And two minutes later, if the enemy agent who is shadowing you knocks on the door, you want to be able to answer it looking like this:

# 1. YOUR HAIR

You can change the way your hair looks by combing it in a different way. You can brush your fringe to one side. You can slick your hair back with water. You can give yourself a new parting.

You can make your hair look grey or white by adding talcum powder to it. (If you give yourself white hair, remember to give yourself eyebrows to match.) The disadvantage of changing the colour of your hair is that you have to wash it to get it back to its normal colour – and that takes time.

You can wear a hat. The more hats you have to wear the better. If you wear a different hat every day, this will confuse the agent who is shadowing you.

## 2. YOUR EYES

You can wear a pair of unusual spectacle frames that don't have any lenses in them. Or you can wear dark glasses. The advantage of dark glasses is that people cannot see your eyes behind them and so no one knows which way you are looking.

## 3. MOUSTACHES AND BEARDS

You can buy very grand false beards and moustaches, but they are expensive, difficult to glue into position and take quite a time to take off.

You can make your own false moustache by using strands of brown or black wool, taped together in the middle of the moustache with scotch tape and then glued to your top lip.

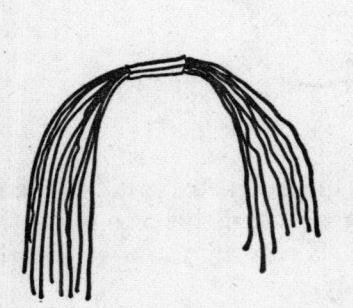

**To make a false beard:** get two pieces of string, one to stretch from ear to ear, and one to make room for your mouth. Tie them like this, with loops to go round your ears:

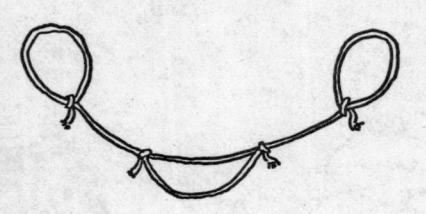

Now get a roll of cotton wool and cut out the shape you want for your beard. Glue the beard to the string:

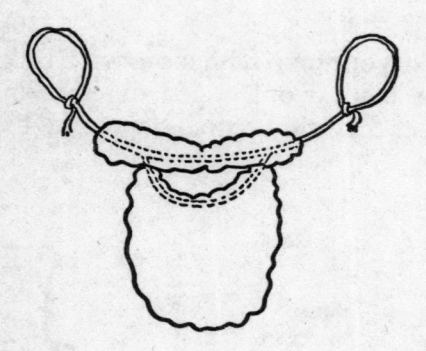

You can wear the beard as it is if you want a white one. If you don't, paint the cotton wool the colour you want it to be with poster paints. Wait until the paint has dried and your beard will be ready.

## 4. YOUR MOUTH

To change the shape of your face put small lumps of cotton wool between your teeth and your cheeks.

## 5. YOUR TEETH

Black out one or more of your front teeth with black crayon and it will look as though you have some teeth missing.

## 6. YOUR FACE

To make your face look paler, very gently rub some talcum powder all over it.

To make your face look darker, very gently rub some cocoa powder all over it. (Be careful not to get the powder on your clothes.)

## 7. YOUR BODY

To give yourself a limp – and to make sure you don't forget to keep on limping or start limping with the wrong foot! – put a pebble inside one of your shoes.

To give yourself a stiff leg – and to make sure you don't forget which leg is supposed to be the stiff one! – tie a ruler to your leg just behind your knee.

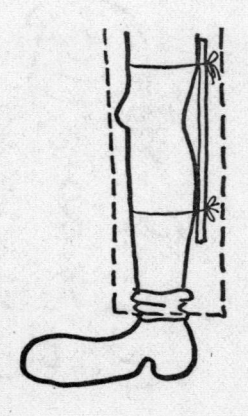

To change the shape of your shoulders, wrap a towel or a small rug around them and then put on your overcoat.

To make you look a lot fatter, tie a pillow or cushion around your stomach and then put on your overcoat:

## 8. YOUR VOICE

There are lots of different ways of disguising your voice. Try each of these methods in turn and see which one suits you best:

- Put on a regional accent and talk as though you came from Ireland or Scotland or Brooklyn or the Deep South.
- Put on a foreign accent and talk as though you came from France or Germany or Italy. (If you know any foreign words, include them in your conversation.)
- Push your lips forward as though you were about to whistle. Talk like this and you'll find your voice sounds very different.
- Stretch your mouth into a really broad grin and try to talk through the smile. It will alter the sound of your voice.
- Frown as hard as you can, with your mouth turned downwards, and talk. Again your voice will sound different.
- Try talking in a very high-pitched voice if normally you have a deep voice. If normally you have a high-pitched voice, try talking in very deep tones.
- Only talk in a whisper and explain that you have a sore throat.
- Put a well-scrubbed pebble into your mouth and talk while sucking it.

If you want to disguise your voice when talking on the telephone, it's much easier because nobody can see what you are doing. Try these methods and see which one you like best:

— Cover the telephone mouthpiece with a clean handkerchief or piece of cloth and speak through it.
— Pinch your nose while you are talking.
— Hold four fingers in your mouth while you are talking.
— Hold a pencil between your teeth while you are talking.

SECRET
WRITING

# INVISIBLE INKS

The best spies are never without a bowl of fruit, a sack of potatoes, a candle, a pint of milk, a glass of water and a larder full of sugar, honey, salt, vinegar and washing soda.

Because you need them to make the very best invisible inks!

If you want to write a secret message, write it in invisible ink. And write your invisible message on a piece of paper that already has a visible message written on it. If you send someone a sheet of paper with nothing on it, that looks fishy. Nobody bothers to send blank pieces of paper! But if you send an ordinary-looking letter to someone, between the lines of which you have written your secret message in invisible ink, an enemy agent finding the letter will think it is as innocent as it looks and won't start examining it closely to see if it contains a secret message written in invisible ink. A blank sheet of paper arouses suspicions. An everyday letter doesn't.

> Dear Charlie,
>     I hope you can come to tea with me on Saturday. We will have lots to eat and it should be great fun. Bring Jerry along too.
>         Yours truly,
>         Benny.
>
> MEET ME TONIGHT AT THE SECRET HUT

To make sure that the person to whom you are sending your message knows it contains a secret message written in invisible ink and to tell him which ink you have used so that he knows how to develop the message and read it, you must sign your letter in a certain way that will show him what's going on but won't arouse any suspicions should the letter fall into enemy hands.

| | | |
|---|---|---|
| Yours truly | = | orange |
| Yours sincerely | = | lemon |
| Yours faithfully | = | grapefruit |
| Yours ever | = | potato |
| Yours always | = | apple |
| Yours | = | pear |
| Yours affectionately | = | sugar |
| Yours very truly | = | honey |
| With best wishes | = | salt |
| With kind regards | = | washing soda |
| With love | = | milk |
| With much love | = | vinegar |
| With lots of love | = | candle wax |
| With love and kisses | = | waters |

On the next few pages fourteen different invisible inks are described. You can indicate which of the fourteen you have used by ending your letter in one of fourteen different ways:

## INVISIBLE INKS

**WHAT YOU NEED:** Orange or Lemon or Grapefruit.

**METHOD:** Squeeze the juice into a teaspoon or an egg-cup. Dip the clean end of a used matchstick into the juice and use the matchstick as a pen and the juice as ink.

**TO DEVELOP:** To develop the message, hold it over a source of heat like a radiator or a light bulb (but do be sure you don't burn yourself). The writing will appear, now brown in colour.

**WHAT YOU NEED:** Potato or Apple or Pear.

**METHOD:** Cut the vegetable or fruit in half and scoop out a hole in the middle to use as your ink-well. With the blade of a knife, scrape the vegetable or fruit juice into the well in the middle. Dip your clean matchstick into the juice and write your message.

**TO DEVELOP:** Hold the message over a source of heat. The writing will appear, now brown in colour.

**WHAT YOU NEED:** Sugar or Honey or Salt or Washing Soda.

**METHOD:** Fill a glass with water and to the water add one teaspoon of sugar (or one teaspoon of one of the other substances). Use the mixture of sugar and water as your ink.

**TO DEVELOP:** Hold the message over a source of heat. The writing will soon appear, again brown in colour.

**WHAT YOU NEED:** Milk or Vinegar.

**METHOD:** Pour a little milk or vinegar into a glass and use them as inks without diluting them at all.

**TO DEVELOP:** Hold the message over a source of heat, and the message will appear.

**WHAT YOU NEED:** A Candle and Ink.

**METHOD:** Write your message with your special candle-pencil.

**TO DEVELOP:** Instead of covering the paper on which the message is written with powder, cover it with the ink wash. Since wax is waterproof, the rest of the paper will become the colour of the ink-wash, and the message will stand out clearly.

**WHAT YOU NEED:** A Candle and Powder.

**METHOD:** Turn an ordinary, colourless wax candle into a special secret writing pencil, by cutting off the end of the candle, pulling out the wick and then sharpening the point of the candle as you would sharpen a pencil. Now write your message with the candle-pencil.

**TO DEVELOP:** Sprinkle powder over the piece of paper on which the invisible message has been written. The powder will cling to the wax writing and so the message will appear.

**WHAT YOU NEED:** Water and Ink.

**METHOD:** Fill a glass with water and use the plain water as ink. Do not send the message off until you are quite sure your water has dried.

**TO DEVELOP:** Add one teaspoon of ink to four teaspoons of ordinary water and stir. Use this solution as a wash and brush it lightly over the whole of the piece of paper on which the secret message has been written. The message will then appear, slightly darker than the rest of the ink-washed paper.

# CODES & CIPHERS

What most people call **CODES** are really **CIPHERS**. The **CIPHERS** you will find on the next few pages have all been used by secret agents in the past.

**Easy Ciphers**

**Not-so-Easy Ciphers** =

= **Difficult ciphers**

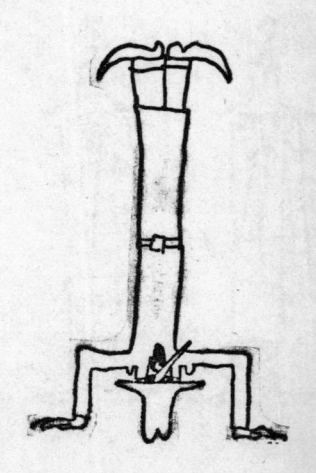

# LETTER CIPHER: WORDS SPLIT

Take your message:

**MISTER BIG IS ARRIVING ON WEDNESDAY. PREPARE TO ATTACK**

And divide the words up in a different way:

**MIST ERBI GISAR RIVI NGONW ED NESDA YP REPA RET OAT TACK**

To make sure you understand how the Words Split Cipher works, try to decipher this secret message:

**IA MBE INGT RAIL EDAN DNE EDHE L PUR GENT LY**

Secret message deciphered:

**I AM BEING TRAILED AND NEED HELP URGENTLY**

# LETTER CIPHER: PHONEY FIRSTS

Take your message:

**WE ARE CLOSING IN ON SPY MASTER FELIX**

Divide the words up in a different way and add a false first letter to every word, like this:

**OWE HARE ACLO USING TIN SONS APYM CAST HER OF ME FLIX**

To make sure you understand how the Phoney Firsts Cipher works – because it's a tough one – try deciphering this secret message:

**TWEH RAVE AB CROK HEN IT WHEC PODE**

Secret message deciphered:

**WE HAVE BROKEN THE CODE**

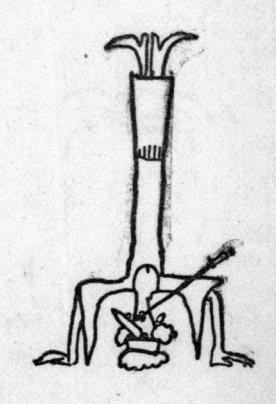

# LETTER CIPHER: PHONEY LASTS

Take your message:

**NEW COURIER ARRIVING NEW YORK TOMORROW**

Divide the words up in a different way and add a false *last* letter to every word, like this:

**NET WCOUP RIEF RART RIVIM NGNJ EWYP ORKI TOMS ORRD OWE**

And to make sure you understand exactly how the Phoney Lasts Cipher works, here is a secret message for you to decipher:

**LEZ TUSMER ETAD TMIH DNIGK HTO**

Secret message deciphered:

LET US MEET AT MIDNIGHT

# LETTER CIPHER: SDROW

Take your message:

**WE NEED MORE SUPPLIES BY TONIGHT**

And write each word backwards, like this:

**EW DEEN EROM SEILPPUS YB THGINOT**

The cipher gets its name because sdrow is words spelt backwards! To make sure you have mastered the Sdrow Cipher, see how quickly you can decipher this secret message:

**EW TSUM TEEM YB EHT TSOP ECIFFO**

Secret message deciphered:

**WE MUST MEET BY THE POST OFFICE**

# LETTER CIPHER: SEGASSEM

Take your message:

**YOU CAN EXPECT THE ATTACK ANYTIME NOW**

And write the whole message backwards, dividing up the words in a different way:

**WONE MITY NAKC ATTAEH TTC EPXEN ACU OY**

Segassem is, of course, messages written backwards, and to find out if you have understood the way the Segassem Cipher works, try to decipher this secret message:

**ROODT NOR FEHTY BE GAS SEMT XE NRU OYEV AEL**

Secret message deciphered:

LEAVE YOUR NEXT
MESSAGE BY THE
FRONT DOOR

*(shown upside down)*

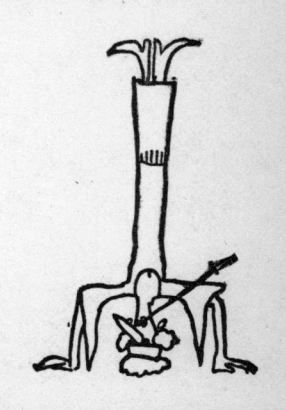

# LETTER CIPHER: SWAP

Take your message:

**THE PARCEL HAS ARRIVED SAFELY**

Begin by dividing up the message into groups of four letters, like this:

**THEP ARCE LHAS ARRI VEDS AFEL Y**

Now swap the last letter of one word with the first letter of the next word, so that your message ends up looking like this:

**THEA PRCL EHAA SRRV IEDA SFEY L**

This is a truly tough one to crack, so don't be surprised if it takes you quite a time to decipher this secret message:

**BEAT THEO HUSB EYSX ITOI NGHT**

Secret message deciphered:

**BE AT THE HOUSE BY SIX TONIGHT.**

# LETTER CIPHER: CAESAR'S CIPHER

The great Roman general Julius Caesar communicated with his officers by means of a special cipher which was already old when he was young, but which has been named after him all the same. In Caesar's Cipher each letter of the alphabet is replaced by the letter that comes three places before it, like this:

| *Alphabet* | *Cipher* |
|:---:|:---:|
| A | X |
| B | Y |
| C | Z |
| D | A |
| E | B |
| F | C |
| G | D |
| H | E |
| I | F |
| J | G |
| K | H |
| L | I |
| M | J |
| N | K |
| O | L |
| P | M |
| Q | N |
| R | O |
| S | P |
| T | Q |
| U | R |
| V | S |
| W | T |
| X | U |
| Y | V |
| Z | W |

To see the cipher in action, have a go at putting this message into Caesar's Cipher:

**CAESAR'S TROOPS HAVE LANDED IN EGYPT**

And to find out if you really know how Caesar's Cipher works, try deciphering this secret message:

**OLJB TXP KLQ YRFIQ FK X AXV**

The message in Caesar's Cipher:

**ZXBPXO'P QOLLMP EXSB IXKABA FK BDVMQ**

Secret message deciphered:

**ROME WAS NOT BUILT IN A DAY**

# LETTER CIPHERS: ALPHABETS

The idea behind Julius Caesar's Cipher is a very simple one, but deciphering messages written in the cipher still isn't easy. Putting the letters of the alphabet in a different order is a clever way of creating a cipher and it would take even a skilled code-cracker quite a time to decipher any of these four famous Alphabet Ciphers:

1. Put the alphabet in reverse, so that A becomes Z, B becomes Y, C becomes X, D becomes W, and so on.

2. Put the five vowels first then list the rest of the alphabet, so that A becomes A, B becomes E, C becomes I, F becomes B, and so on.

3. Put all the even letters of the alphabet first (B because it's second, D because it's fourth, F because it's sixth, and so on), followed by all the uneven letters of the alphabet (A because it's first, C because it's third, E because it's fifth, and so on).

4. Put all the letters of the alphabet that contain no curved lines when written as capitals first (A, E, F, H, I, K, L, M, N, T, V, W, X, Y, Z), followed by the remaining letters of the alphabet.

Here is the alphabet, with cipher equivalents for the four Alphabet Ciphers:

| Real letter | Cipher 1 | Cipher 2 | Cipher 3 | Cipher 4 |
|---|---|---|---|---|
| A | Z | A | B | A |
| B | Y | E | D | E |
| C | X | I | F | F |
| D | W | O | H | H |
| E | V | U | J | I |
| F | U | B | L | K |
| G | T | C | N | L |
| H | S | D | P | M |
| I | R | F | R | N |
| J | Q | G | T | T |
| K | P | H | V | V |
| L | O | J | X | W |
| M | N | K | Z | X |
| N | M | L | A | Y |
| O | L | M | C | Z |
| P | K | N | E | B |
| Q | J | P | G | C |
| R | I | Q | I | D |
| S | H | R | K | G |
| T | G | S | M | J |
| U | F | T | O | O |
| V | E | V | Q | P |
| W | D | W | S | Q |
| X | C | X | U | R |
| Y | B | Y | W | S |
| Z | A | Z | Y | U |

When you think you have really mastered these Alphabet Ciphers, you can devise an Alphabet Cipher of your own. To make sure you know how they work, see how long it takes you to work out which of the four ciphers this message is in and what it means:

**GSV HVXIVG RH LFG**

Secret message deciphered:

**THE SECRET IS OUT**

It is written in Cipher 1.

# LETTER CIPHER: IN THE BEGINNING

Take your message:

## LEAVE AT ONCE

And use the letters in your message to write another message in which each word begins with a letter from your secret message, like this:

## LOCK EVERYTHING AWAY. VALUABLE EVIDENCE ABOUT TIMOTHY'S ORGANISATION NOW CREATES EMERGENCY

Now see if you can decipher the secret message hidden inside this message:

## DAVID OSBORNE NEVER TOLD MICHAEL IF SECRET SOCIETY TOLD HIM EVERYTHING. TOMORROW'S RAID ABSOLUTELY IMPERATIVE. NERO

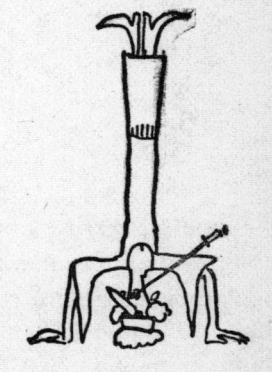

Secret message deciphered:

## DON'T MISS THE TRAIN

# LETTER CIPHER: TYPEWRITER

The letters on the keyboard of a typewriter are not in alphabetical order. To use the Typewriter Cipher you have to know the order in which the letters appear on the keyboard. List them and put the alphabet alongside them and you have found your cipher:

| *Typewriter* | *Alphabet* | *Typewriter* | *Alphabet* |
|---|---|---|---|
| Q | A | F | N |
| W | B | G | O |
| E | C | H | P |
| R | D | J | Q |
| T | E | K | R |
| Y | F | L | S |
| U | G | Z | T |
| I | H | X | U |
| O | I | C | V |
| P | J | V | W |
| A | K | B | X |
| S | L | N | Y |
| D | M | M | Z |

Some typewriters in some countries have the letters in a slightly different order, so take a close look at a local typewriter before you start using the cipher.

Once you have mastered the Typewriter Cipher, it won't take you a minute to decipher this secret message:

**DTTZ DT QZ ZVG ZGRQN**

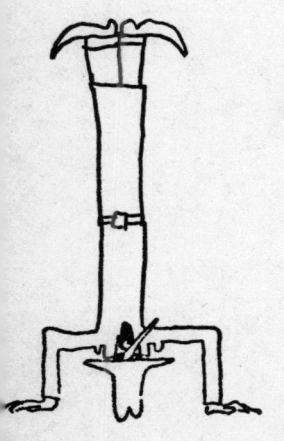

Secret message deciphered:

MEET ME AT
TWO TODAY

# LETTER CIPHER: SOUNDS

To use the Sounds Cipher you must write the word that *sounds* like the letter if there is a word that sounds like the letter. If there isn't, just write the letter.

| *Alphabet* | *Sounds* |
|---|---|
| A | EH |
| B | BEE |
| C | SEA |
| D | DEE |
| E | E |
| F | F |
| G | GEE |
| H | H |
| I | EYE |
| J | JAY |
| K | KAY |
| L | L |
| M | EM |
| N | EN |
| O | OWE |
| P | PEA |
| Q | QUEUE |
| R | OUR |
| S | S |
| T | TEA |
| U | EWE |
| V | V |
| W | DOUBLE EWE |
| X | X |
| Y | WHY |
| Z | Z |

Once you know the Sounds Cipher, you will have no difficulty deciphering this message:

**JAYOWEHEN EYES SEAOWEEMEYEENGEE TEAOWEDEEEHWHY**

Secret message deciphered:

JOHN IS COMING TODAY

# LETTER CIPHER: TREVANION'S CIPHER

According to an old tradition, during the English Civil War, in 1648, one of King Charles's Cavalier officers, Sir John Trevanion, was imprisoned in Colchester Castle and would have been executed there, had he not received the following letter and so been able to escape:

Worthie Sir John:— Hope, that is the beste comfort of the afflicted, cannot much, I feare me, help you now. That I would saye to you, is this only: if ever I may be able to requite that I do owe you, stand not upon asking me. 'Tis not much I can do: but what I can do, bee you verie sure I wille. I knowe that, if dethe comes, if ordinary men fear it, it frights not you, accounting it for a high honour, to have such a rewarde of your loyalty. Pray yet that you may be spared this soe bitter cup. I fear not that you will grudge any sufferings; onlie if bie submission you can turn them away, 'tis the part of a wise man. Tell me, as if you can, to do for you any thinge that you wolde have done. The general goes back on Wednesday. Restinge your servant to command.

R.T.

The prison guard read the letter before giving it to Sir John and could see nothing suspicious about it. Sir John, however, knew that if he read the third letter following every punctuation mark the secret message would be revealed.

Now you know how Trevanion's Cipher works, can you decipher the message that is supposed to have saved his life? We have to say 'that is supposed to have saved his life' because it turns out that the real John Trevanion was fatally wounded at the storming of Bristol in 1643, five years before he is supposed to have escaped from Colchester Castle! Even if Trevanion died in 1643, *someone* sent the secret message to a Cavalier officer in 1648. Nobody knows who. And nobody, except those who know the secret of what is called Trevanion's Cipher, can understand the message. How long did it take you to decipher it?

Secret message deciphered:

**PANEL AT EAST END OF CHAPEL SLIDES**

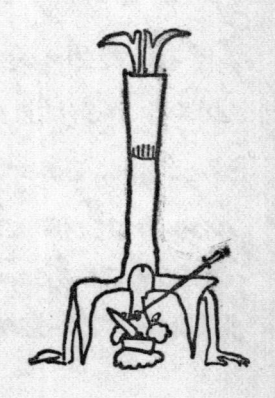

# LETTER CIPHER: RAIL-FENCE

The Rail-Fence Cipher is one of the most famous and useful of all ciphers. Take your message:

**DELIVER THE SECRETS TONIGHT**

And write it on two lines, going up and down, like this:

```
D L V R H S C E S O I H
 E I E T E E R T T N G T
```

Now divide the letters into groups of four, taking the top line first, followed by the second line, and you have put your message into a cipher. If you find you don't have enough letters to put four into the last group, add any letters you like to the last group. These extra letters mean nothing and are called 'nulls'. Here is your message in the Rail-Fence Cipher:

**DLVR HSCE SOIH EIET EERT TNGT**

You don't have to divide the letters into groups of four. You can divide them as you please. For example, can you decipher this secret message:

**EC PN WS AE OX**

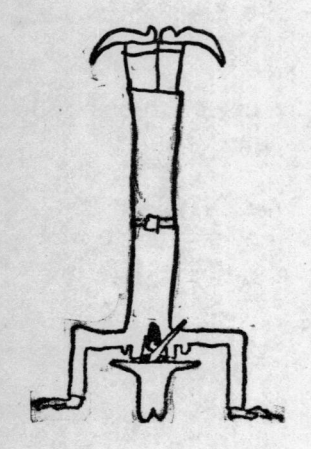

Secret message deciphered:

**ESCAPE NOW** (upside down)

# LETTER CIPHER: COLUMN

The Column Cipher is a close cousin of the Rail-Fence Cipher. To use it you must take your message:

**KAREN KNOWS THE TRUTH**

And write it out in two columns, like this:

```
K  S
A  T
R  H
E  E
N  T
K  R
N  U
O  T
W  H
```

Now, taking the letters row by row, write them out, dividing them into groups of any number, adding 'nulls' to the last group if need be, like this:

**KSATR HEENT KRNUO TWHQZ**

If you have understood the way the Column Cipher works, it won't take you long to decipher this secret message:

**BTE ORN EIA GDH YTS**

Secret message deciphered:

**BE READY TONIGHT**

# LETTER CIPHER: THE BIG BOX

Draw a big box like this one, containing at least twenty-five squares:

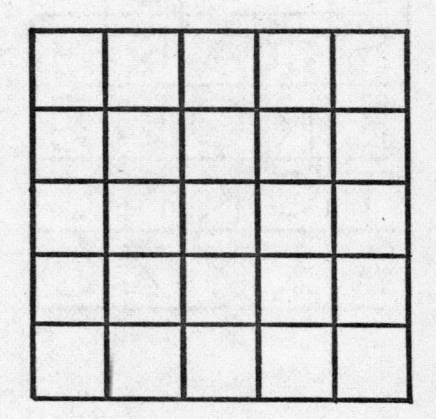

Now write your message inside the box, starting on the top row and working your way down. If your message contains more than twenty-five letters you will need a bigger box. If it contains fewer, fill any empty squares with 'nulls' at the end.

For example, if this is your message:

**JILL IS DANGEROUS TO KNOW**

This is how you will fill in your box, putting 'nulls' into the last four squares:

| J | I | L | L | I |
|---|---|---|---|---|
| S | D | A | N | G |
| E | R | O | U | S |
| T | O | K | N | O |
| W | X | Y | Z | Q |

To write out your secret message you can now take the letters from your Big Box in a number of different ways. The most obvious is to take each of the five columns in turn, like this:

**JSETW IDROX LAOKY LNUNZ IGSOQ**

But you can start in almost any one of the twenty-five squares and take the letters in whatever order you please. Here are four alternative routes, which will give you the same secret message written in four different ways:

**Route 1**

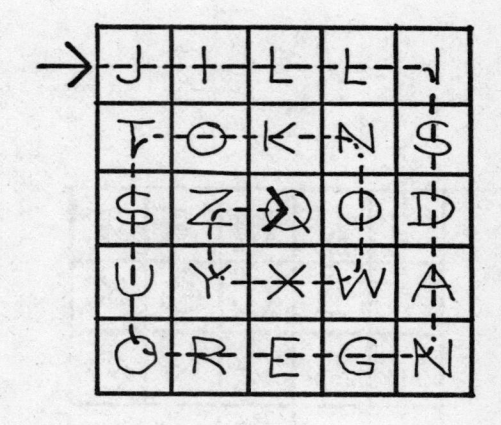

**Route 2**

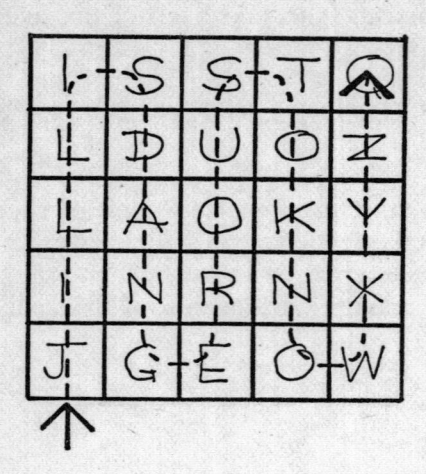

| I | S | S | T | Q |
|---|---|---|---|---|
| L | D | U | O | N |
| L | A | O | K | Y |
| I | N | R | N | X |
| J | G | E | O | W |

**Route 3**

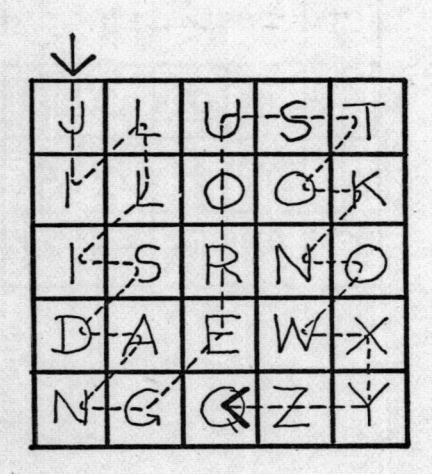

| U | L | U | S | T |
|---|---|---|---|---|
| I | L | O | O | K |
| I | S | R | N | O |
| D | A | E | W | X |
| N | G | Q | Z | Y |

80

# Route 4

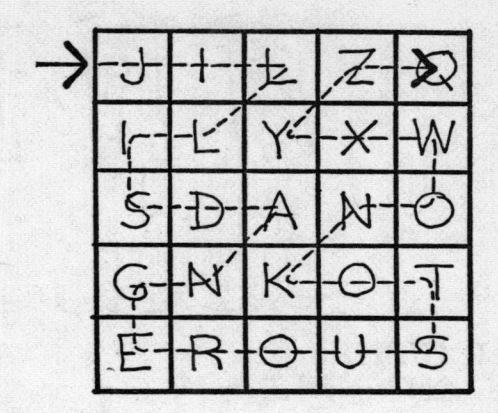

|   |   |   |   |   |
|---|---|---|---|---|
| J | I | L | Z | Q |
| I | L | Y | X | W |
| S | D | A | N | O |
| G | N | K | O | T |
| E | R | O | U | S |

Check to see if you have mastered the Big Box Cipher by trying to work out which of the four routes has been followed to make the secret message read:

**WTESJ XORDI YKOAL ZNUNL QOSGI**

The secret route:

Route number 2

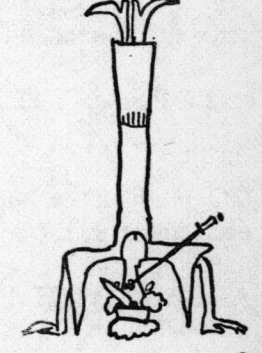

## LETTER CIPHER:
## A-NULL AND NULL-A

Take your message:

### LEAVE FOR MOSCOW AT ONCE

And either put a 'null' in front of every letter or after every letter. Since a 'null' is a letter that doesn't mean anything, when you need a 'null' you can use any letter you like. When using the A-Null Cipher you put a null after each letter in the message, like this:

### LOERANVTEI FROMRE MIOXSACROPWZ AITR OLNMCQEK

When using the Null-A Cipher you put a null in front of each letter in the message, like this:

### ALBERAIVTE IFYOAR UMPOISTCBOOW HALT HORNICVE

To make life a bit more complicated for the enemy, you can divide the letters up into different groups, like this:

**LOER ANVT EIFR OMRE MIOX SACR OPWZ
AITR OLNM CQEK**

or like this:

**ALB ERAIVT EIF YOARUM POI STCBOO WHA
LTHORN ICV E**

## LETTER CIPHER: VOWEL-PLUS

This cipher works in the same way as the A-Null Cipher, except that you only add 'nulls' after the five vowels, **A, E, I, O, U**, and the letter **Y**, and your nulls can be any letters of the alphabet except for **A, E, I, O, U** and **Y**. For example, here is your message:

**YOU MUST RELEASE THE PRISONER**

And here it is written with the Vowel-Plus Cipher:

**YHOKUM MUDST REWLESASSES THEM PRIFSOVNEXR**

To see how well you have managed to master the A-Null, Null-A and Vowel-Plus Cipher, try to work out in which of the three ciphers this secret message is written and what it means. Remember that the letters may not be grouped as words.

**DAXN GEPROLUKSS PYZH AT SAD RRIBVEW D IP NTOT WN**

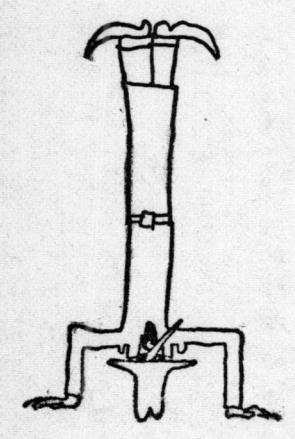

Secret message deciphered:

**DANGEROUS SPY HAS ARRIVED IN TOWN**

The message was written with the Vowel-Plus Cipher.

# NUMBER CIPHER:
123

The most common Number Cipher has the twenty-six letters of the alphabet indicated by the numbers 1 to 26:

| Letter | Number |
|--------|--------|
| A | 1 |
| B | 2 |
| C | 3 |
| D | 4 |
| E | 5 |
| F | 6 |
| G | 7 |
| H | 8 |
| I | 9 |
| J | 10 |
| K | 11 |
| L | 12 |
| M | 13 |
| N | 14 |
| O | 15 |
| P | 16 |
| Q | 17 |
| R | 18 |
| S | 19 |
| T | 20 |
| U | 21 |
| V | 22 |
| W | 23 |
| X | 24 |
| Y | 25 |
| Z | 26 |

Knowing how the 123 Cipher works, can you decipher this secret message:

2085 11525 919 914 2085 1192038514

Secret message deciphered:

THE KITCHEN
THE KEY IS IN
(upside down)

# NUMBER CIPHER: ANY NUMBER

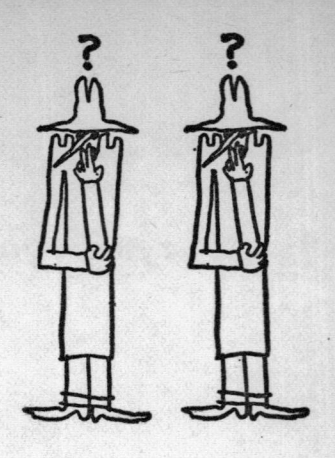

The 123 Cipher is easy to operate and simple to decipher. The Any Number Cipher isn't, because when you use it you can start with any number you like, so that A can be 2 or 17 or 222 or any of an infinite number of numbers. On the opposite page are three of the possible Any Number Ciphers.

Here is a secret message written in one of these three Any Number Ciphers. Which one? And what does the message say?

172828 2535 28313536

Secret message deciphered:

ALL IS LOST.

| Letter | Number | Number | Number |
|--------|--------|--------|--------|
| A | 2  | 17 | 222 |
| B | 3  | 18 | 223 |
| C | 4  | 19 | 224 |
| D | 5  | 20 | 225 |
| E | 6  | 21 | 226 |
| F | 7  | 22 | 227 |
| G | 8  | 23 | 228 |
| H | 9  | 24 | 229 |
| I | 10 | 25 | 230 |
| J | 11 | 26 | 231 |
| K | 12 | 27 | 232 |
| L | 13 | 28 | 234 |
| M | 14 | 29 | 235 |
| N | 15 | 30 | 236 |
| O | 16 | 31 | 237 |
| P | 17 | 32 | 238 |
| Q | 18 | 33 | 239 |
| R | 19 | 34 | 240 |
| S | 20 | 35 | 241 |
| T | 21 | 36 | 242 |
| U | 22 | 37 | 243 |
| V | 23 | 38 | 244 |
| W | 24 | 39 | 245 |
| X | 25 | 40 | 246 |
| Y | 26 | 41 | 247 |
| Z | 27 | 42 | 248 |

The message was written using the second Any Number Cipher.

# NUMBER CIPHER: REVERSE ORDER

Here is a Number Cipher very like the 123 Cipher, except that you take the alphabet in reverse order so that Z is 1 and A is 26, like this:

| Letter | Number |
|--------|--------|
| A | 26 |
| B | 25 |
| C | 24 |
| D | 23 |
| E | 22 |
| F | 21 |
| G | 20 |
| H | 19 |
| I | 18 |
| J | 17 |
| K | 16 |
| L | 15 |
| M | 14 |
| N | 13 |
| O | 12 |
| P | 11 |
| Q | 10 |
| R | 9 |
| S | 8 |
| T | 7 |
| U | 6 |
| V | 5 |
| W | 4 |
| X | 3 |
| Y | 2 |
| Z | 1 |

Now you know how the Reverse Order Cipher operates, see how long it takes you to decipher this secret message:

**26142 19268 25222213 2426620197**

Secret message deciphered:

AMY HAS
BEEN CAUGHT

# NUMBER CIPHER: THE POPULARITY POLL

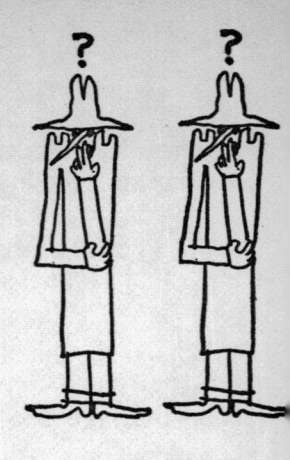

In spoken and written English, some letters of the alphabet are used much more often than others. **E, T** and **A**, for example, are the three most frequently used letters of the alphabet, and **J, Q** and **Z** are the three letters that occur least often. Knowing which letters are likely to be used the most and which are likely to be used the least should help you crack all kinds of ciphers and the order of popularity of the letters can also be used as the basis of a very difficult Number Cipher.

On the opposite page are the twenty-six letters of the alphabet in their order of popularity.

When you are trying to decipher secret messages, this popularity poll will help you because if you find one letter or number or sign occurring much more often than others it is more likely to be one of the top ten letters of the alphabet than one of the bottom ones. Roughly speaking, in every hundred letters used in written or spoken English, **E** occurs thirteen times, **T** ten times, **A** and **O** eight times, **N** and **R** seven times, **I** and **S** six times, **H** five times, **D** four times, **L, F, C** and **M** three times, **U, G, Y** and **P** twice, and **W, B, V, K, X, J, Q** and **Z** less than twice. The figures have been rounded up or down, but the order in which they appear in the popularity poll is the correct one.

| Position | Letter |
|---|---|
| 1 | E |
| 2 | T |
| 3 | A |
| 4 | O |
| 5 | N |
| 6 | R |
| 7 | I |
| 8 | S |
| 9 | H |
| 10 | D |
| 11 | L |
| 12 | F |
| 13 | C |
| 14 | M |
| 15 | U |
| 16 | G |
| 17 | Y |
| 18 | P |
| 19 | W |
| 20 | B |
| 21 | V |
| 22 | K |
| 23 | X |
| 24 | J |
| 25 | Q |
| 26 | Z |

When trying to break a cipher, it is also worth knowing the most frequently used words in the English language. Here are the Top Thirty Words: they are likely to occur more often in written English than other words, so that when you are deciphering a message they are ones to look out for:

| | |
|---|---|
| THE | HE |
| OF | BE |
| AND | NOT |
| TO | BY |
| A | BUT |
| IN | HAVE |
| THAT | YOU |
| IS | WHICH |
| I | ARE |
| IT | ON |
| FOR | OR |
| AS | HER |
| WITH | HAD |
| WAS | AT |
| HIS | FROM |

Once you have learnt the list of Top Thirty Words and have mastered the order of popularity of the letters of the alphabet, try using the Popularity Poll Cipher. With this cipher each letter of the alphabet is given a number equivalent to its position in the poll, so that E is 1, A is 3, B is 20, C is 13, Z is 26, and so on. Here is a message written with the Popularity Poll Cipher. What does it say?

    174156 134101 53141 78 144522117

Secret message deciphered:

YOUR CODE NAME
IS MONKEY

# NUMBER CIPHER: ROMAN CIPHER

The Roman Cipher is just like the 123 Cipher, except that instead of using Arabic numerals (1, 2, 3, 4, 5, and so on) you use Roman numerals:

| Letter | Number |
|--------|--------|
| A | I |
| B | II |
| C | III |
| D | IV |
| E | V |
| F | VI |
| G | VII |
| H | VIII |
| I | IX |
| J | X |
| K | XI |
| L | XII |
| M | XIII |
| N | XIV |
| O | XV |
| P | XVI |
| Q | XVII |
| R | XVIII |
| S | XIX |
| T | XX |
| U | XXI |
| V | XXII |
| W | XXIII |
| X | XXIV |
| Y | XXV |
| Z | XXVI |

To decipher a secret message written with the Roman Cipher calls for lots of patience, because all those Xs keep on getting muddled up, but it can be done. Have a go:

XIIIXXV XVIXVIIIIXXIXXVXIVVXVIII VIIIIXIX
VXIXIIIIXVIVIV

Secret message deciphered:

MY PRISONER
HAS ESCAPED

(inverted)

# SIGN CIPHER: MUSICAL NOTES

This is a very special Sign Cipher that would fool most people, unless they happen to be able to read music and could tell that the notes weren't *real* notes at all! With the Musical Notes Cipher, letters and numbers are represented by different notes, like this:

If you wrote a message like this one using the Musical Notes Cipher, someone who couldn't read music would probably think it was a delightful composition by Mozart or Chopin or Bach or Beethoven! They wouldn't realize that it was, in fact, a very secret message. Can you decipher it?

Secret message deciphered:

I AM NOW 13 (upside down)

# SIGN CIPHER: MORSE CODE

The Morse Code, invented by Samuel Morse in 1838, isn't really a code at all. It's a cipher. And it isn't a very secret cipher because it is known to millions of people all round the world. All the same, no self-respecting spy or secret agent could admit to *not* knowing the Morse Code, so if you don't know it yet, learn it now!

| | | |
|---|---|---|
| A .− | M −− | Y −.−− |
| B −... | N −. | Z −−.. |
| C −.−. | O −−− | 1 .−−−− |
| D −.. | P .−−. | 2 ..−−− |
| E . | Q −−.− | 3 ...−− |
| F ..−. | R .−. | 4 ....− |
| G −−. | S ... | 5 ..... |
| H .... | T − | 6 −.... |
| I .. | U ..− | 7 −−... |
| J .−−− | V ...− | 8 −−−.. |
| K −.− | W .−− | 9 −−−−. |
| L .−.. | X −..− | 0 −−−−− |

When writing Morse, a short horizontal line shows the end of a letter (be sure not to confuse it with a dash), and a short horizontal line with a break in it shows the end of a word. See if you can decipher this message:

The Morse Code was invented for sending messages by telegraph and was never intended to be used for written messages. If you can whistle or you own a whistle you can send messages by Morse Code by giving a short whistle to represent the dots and a longer whistle to represent the dashes.

Instead of writing Morse Code with dots and dashes, you can write it so that the dots are represented by low peaks and the dashes are represented by high ones. Here is the same message written with high and low peaks instead of dashes and dots:

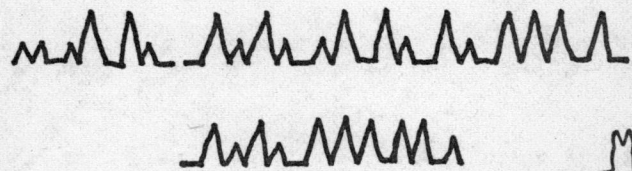

Secret message deciphered:

IAN CANNOT COME

# SIGN CIPHER: SEMAPHORE

The Semaphore Cipher is another one you should know, even though it is known to millions. Traditionally, Semaphore messages are sent by someone holding two flags in different positions to indicate different letters. When writing Semaphore, you mark the flag positions with two lines at different angles, like this:

| | | | | | | | |
|---|---|---|---|---|---|---|---|
| A | ⤭ 1 | H | ⤳ 8 | O | ⤲ | V | ⬊ |
| B | ⤵ 2 | I | ⩺ 9 | P | ⤶ | W | ⤶ |
| C | ⤸ 3 | J | ⌐ | Q | ⤵ | X | ⟨ |
| D | ⤈ 4 | K | ⤿ | R | ⟝ | Y | ⬎ |
| E | ⤏ 5 | L | ⁄ | S | ⤸ | Z | ⤇ |
| F | ⊤ 6 | M | ⤸ | T | ⤋ | | |
| G | ⤊ 7 | N | ⋀ | U | ⋁ | | |

Here is a Semaphore Cipher message for you to decipher as quickly as you can:

The truly great master spies will use Semaphore and Morse, but not in the straightforward way that has just been described. They will either use the Semaphore and Morse signs to represent the ordinary alphabet and then disguise that alphabet by using one of the Letter Ciphers described between pages 58 and 89, *or* they will take the Semaphore and Morse signs and give them new meanings, so that the Semaphore **V** won't be U at all and the Morse **— — —** won't be O any more. If you feel you are a master spy in the making, you can try using Morse and Semaphore in a new and very secret cipher of your own.

Secret message deciphered:

TOM IS OUR
NEW SPY

# SIGN CIPHER: PIG-PEN

No, pigs don't write with pens: they use typewriters. And the Pig-pen Cipher has got nothing to do with pigs and very little to do with pens, except the sort you keep animals in. Begin by drawing four funny-looking animal pens:

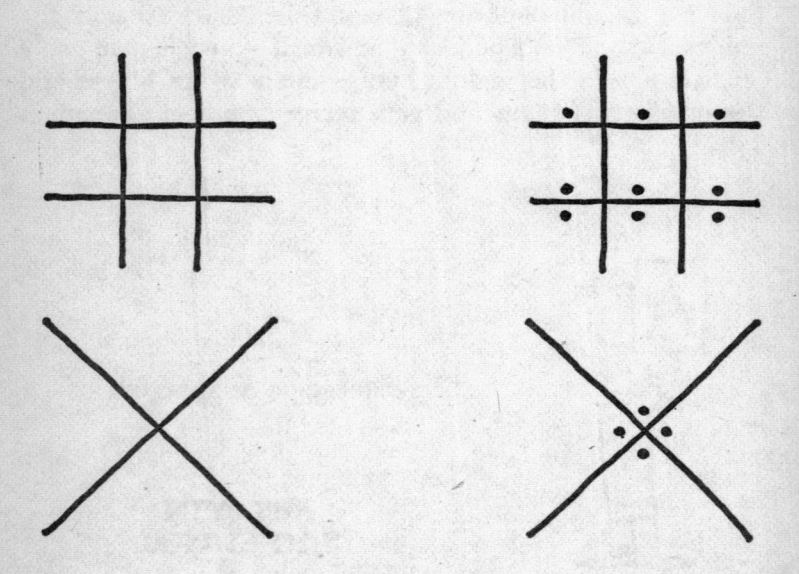

Now add the twenty-six letters of the alphabet, like this:

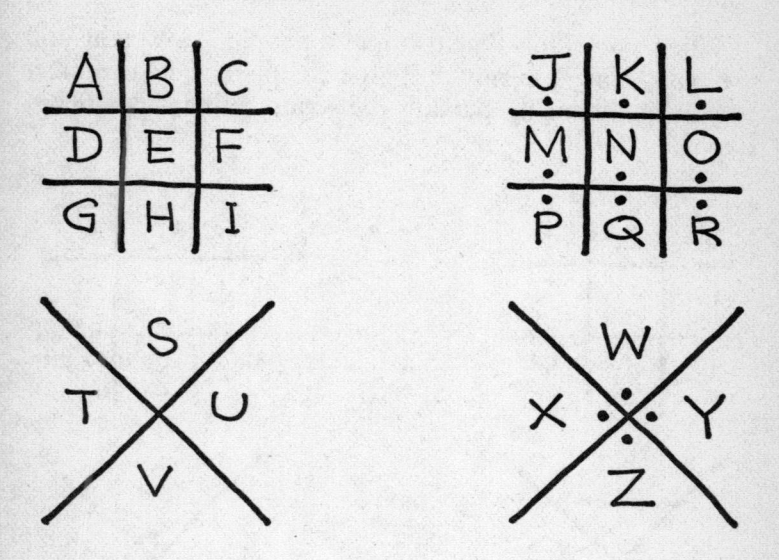

And that, believe it or not, is all there is to the Pig-pen Cipher. If you are still confused, watch how the word SPYMASTER can be written in the cipher:

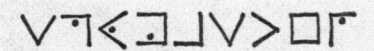

And see if you can decipher this Pig-pen message:

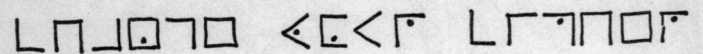

⌐⊓⌐⊡⌐⊡   ⟨⊡⟨⌐   ⌐⌐⊓⊡⌐

When you think that too many people know that you are using the traditional Pig-pen Cipher, you can start to confuse them by putting the letters in new positions, like this:

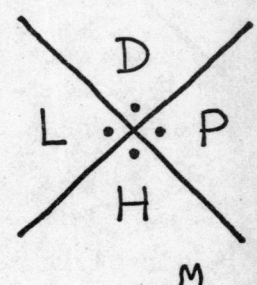

```
A | E | I        B | F | J
M | Q | S        N | R | T
U | W | Y        V | X | Z
```

(with the second grid having dots in each cell)

```
    C              D
K ✕ O          L ✕ P
    G              H
```

(with the second X having dots)

Secret message deciphered:

CHANGE YOUR CIPHER

# SIGN CIPHER: TYPEWRITER

If you can get hold of a typewriter, here is a cipher you can invent for yourself, using the signs and symbols on the typewriter to represent different letters, like this:

| Letter | Sign |
|--------|------|
| A | * |
| B | " |
| C | / |
| D | @ |
| E | ! |
| F | — |
| G | & |
| H | ' |
| I | ( |
| J | ) |
| K | ¼ |
| L | + |
| M | ? |
| N | ⅓ |
| O | : |
| P | , |
| Q | % |
| R | ¾ |
| S | = |
| T | - |
| U | ; |
| V | ⅔ |
| W | ½ |
| X | . |
| Y | !!! |
| Z | ... |

The Typewriter Cipher is a very useful one indeed, because very few people seeing this written on a scrap of paper

$$!=/*,!\quad *-\quad :\tfrac{1}{3}/!$$

would think for a moment that it could possibly mean

### ESCAPE AT ONCE

When you use the Typewriter Cipher, remember not to include any real punctuation marks in your message or no one will ever be able to decipher it!

See how long it takes you to decipher this Typewriter message:

$$*+(/!\quad (=\quad *\quad ,\tfrac{3}{4}(=:\tfrac{1}{3}!\tfrac{3}{4}$$

Secret message deciphered:

ALICE IS A PRISONER

# SIGN CIPHER: DO-IT-YOURSELF

If you don't like the Pig-pen, Morse and Semaphore Ciphers and can't get hold of a typewriter, why don't you invent a Sign Cipher of your own, like these ones.

# CODES

Codes are very different from ciphers. Codes aren't based on alphabets, with one letter or sign or number representing A or B or C or any other letter. Codes use words or groups of letters or numbers or symbols to represent other words, not in a systematic way, just in a secret way known only to the sender of the message and the person who receives it. It's because codes aren't based on any system, like an alphabet, that they are much more difficult to crack than ciphers are to decipher.

For example, if you wanted to send this message using a cipher:

**WE ARE READY TO ATTACK LONDON**

you would have to write it out with a cipher representing each letter. With a code, this one word could represent the whole message:

**APRICOT**

A Code Book is really rather like a dictionary, in which one short word has a meaning that takes several words to explain. For example, in one code **APRIL FOOL** could mean **THE MASTER SPY HAS BEEN UNCOVERED ESCAPE AS QUICKLY AS YOU CAN** but in another code the same words, **APRIL FOOL**, could mean **ALL IS WELL AND I WILL REPORT AGAIN AT THE SAME TIME TO-MORROW.**

If you want to invent a code of your own, you should begin by writing out all the messages you think you might need to send in code and then think of code words (or numbers or letters or signs) to represent the messages – like this:

| Message | Code Word |
|---|---|
| I AM COMING NOW | BUMBLEBEE |
| I AM GOING TO STAY HERE | RADIO |
| COME AND GET ME | DAFFODIL |
| I AM PRISONER | SNOOPY |
| HELP! | RHINOCEROS |
| I AM GETTING HUNGRY | CORK |
| WHAT TIME IS IT? | BUTTERFLY |
| ARE YOU ALONE? | RIVER |
| WE MUST REPORT TO MASTER SPY AT ONCE | CHICAGO |
| IS OUR ESCAPE ROUTE CLEAR? | JOURNEY |
| HAVE YOU GOT THE SUPPLIES? | CUCUMBER |
| I AM GOING INDOORS NOW TO HAVE LUNCH | CONCORDE |

If you make up code words for your own messages, you will only be able to send messages for which you have already found a code word. For example, if you only had the dozen messages listed above in your personal Code Book, you could send a message to say **I AM COMING NOW** by writing the word **BUMBLEBEE**, but you couldn't send a message saying **I AM NOT COMING NOW** because you have no code word for that particular message!

To save you making your own Code Book, thinking of all the messages you might ever want to send and finding code words for them, you could use a book that already exists. Secret agents and spies around the world regularly use famous books as their own code books, the most frequently used being dictionaries and plays by William Shakespeare. For example, this message might mean nothing to you:

1/1 1207/17 613/9 553/30

But to anyone knowing that the code it was written in was based on a certain English dictionary would be able to work out that the message means:

**A SPY IS HERE**

And that's because **1/1** means the first line of the first page and the word listed on the first line of the first page of the dictionary is **A**, and **1207/17** means the seventeenth line on page **1207** where the word listed is **SPY**, and on the ninth line on page **613** you will find the word **IS** and on the thirtieth line on page **553** the word **HERE**!

In the same way, this won't mean much to you:

IIiii8three Ii1two IVi8ofour

But the person who knows that the code is based on William Shakespeare's play *Julius Caesar* will be able to decode the message as:

**COME HOME NOW**

**IIiii8three** stands for Act II, Scene iii, line 8, word three, which is **COME**. **Ii1two** stands for Act I, Scene i, line 1, word two, which is **HOME**. And **IVi80four** stands for Act IV, Scene i, line 80, word four, which is **NOW**!

Sending coded messages is a complicated business and very hard work, but it can be exciting too. Trying to decode messages, when you do not know what the code words mean and do not have a copy of the code book that has been used is almost impossible and can take *years* of effort!

# CODE GRILLES

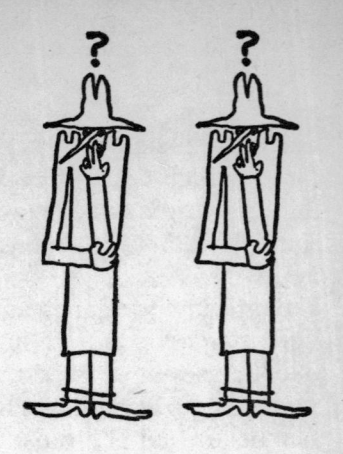

Here is a letter that looks as innocent as a new-born lamb:

> Dear John,
> I do hope you are well. I really must apologise for not writing to you before now, but the holiday has rushed by and I haven't had time to get down to writing any letters. You will be pleased to hear that I used my pocket money this week to buy a record from the new shop at the corner of our street and when you and Jane come and see me next I will play it to you. That's all for now. I hope you and Jane are going to visit me again soon. Do tell her she is always welcome.
> 
> With best wishes,
> Alex
>
> P.S. I do hope this letter doesn't get lost in the post! I sent one to Auntie Jane last September and it never arrived.

Put this cardboard grille over the letter:

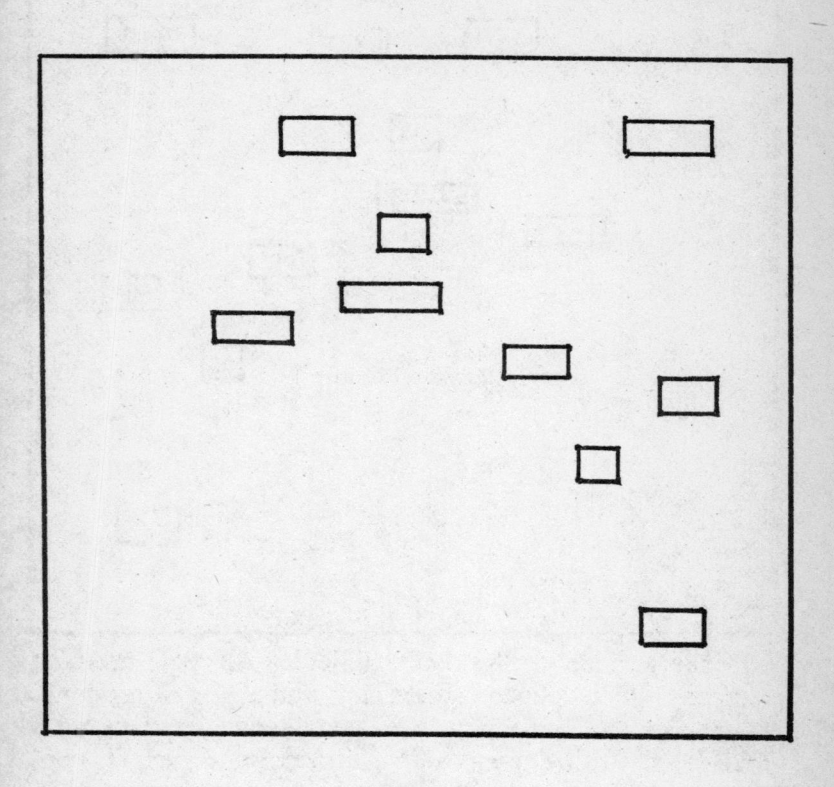

And see how there was much more to the letter than you ever imagined:

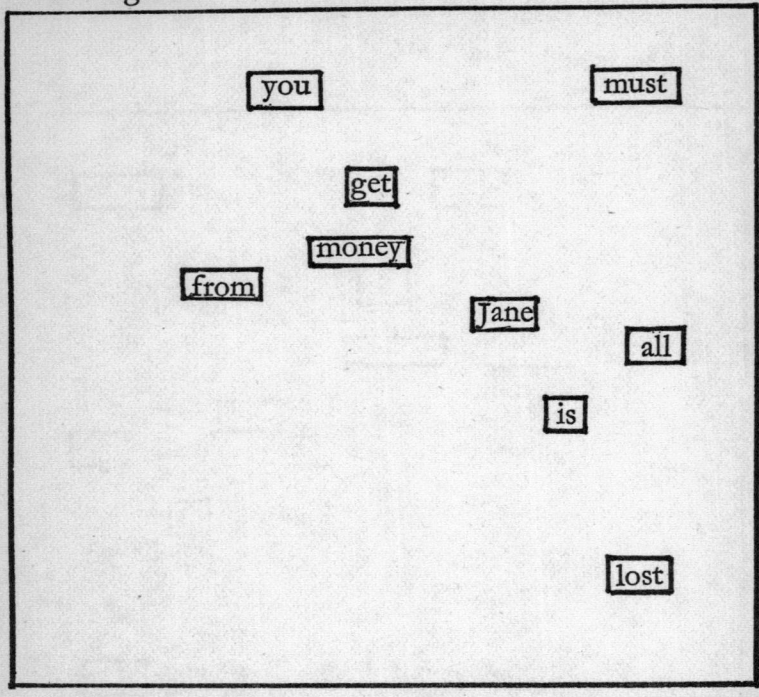

> you    must
>
>     get
>     money
> from
>         Jane
>             all
>             is
>
>
>             lost

Making code grilles isn't difficult. All you need is a piece of thick paper or thin card and a pair of scissors. Cut holes to fit the words in your secret message and then lay the grille over the piece of paper on which you plan to send the message. Fill in the holes with the words in the secret message. Remove the grille and write your innocent letter around the secret words, making it make as much sense as possible. Send the letter to whoever you want to get your secret message and, provided they have a grille like yours, to read the secret message all they have to do is place the grille over the letter and read the words that appear in the holes.

# PIN HOLE CODES

If you want to send this secret message:

**I AM CAUGHT SEND HELP IMMEDIATELY**

all you would need to do is write a letter like this:

> Dear Aunt Alice,
>
> I am writing to thank you for your lovely birthday present. I would have written earlier, but I caught a terrible cold just after my birthday and have been in bed for two weeks. I was really quite ill and my parents had to send for Doctor Johnson who came to see me and was a great help. It was sweet of you to send me the money as well as the present. Don't worry, I won't spend it immediately: I will save up and buy something special later in the year.
>
>                       With love from,
>
>                             Janet.

And under the words **I AM CAUGHT SEND HELP IMMEDIATELY,** mark tiny pin holes. No one will notice them, but the person who gets the letter will be able to hold it up to the light and read the words indicated by the holes!

If you think pin holes are too obvious (and they will be unless you use a very small pin!) you can underline the words of the message in invisible ink.

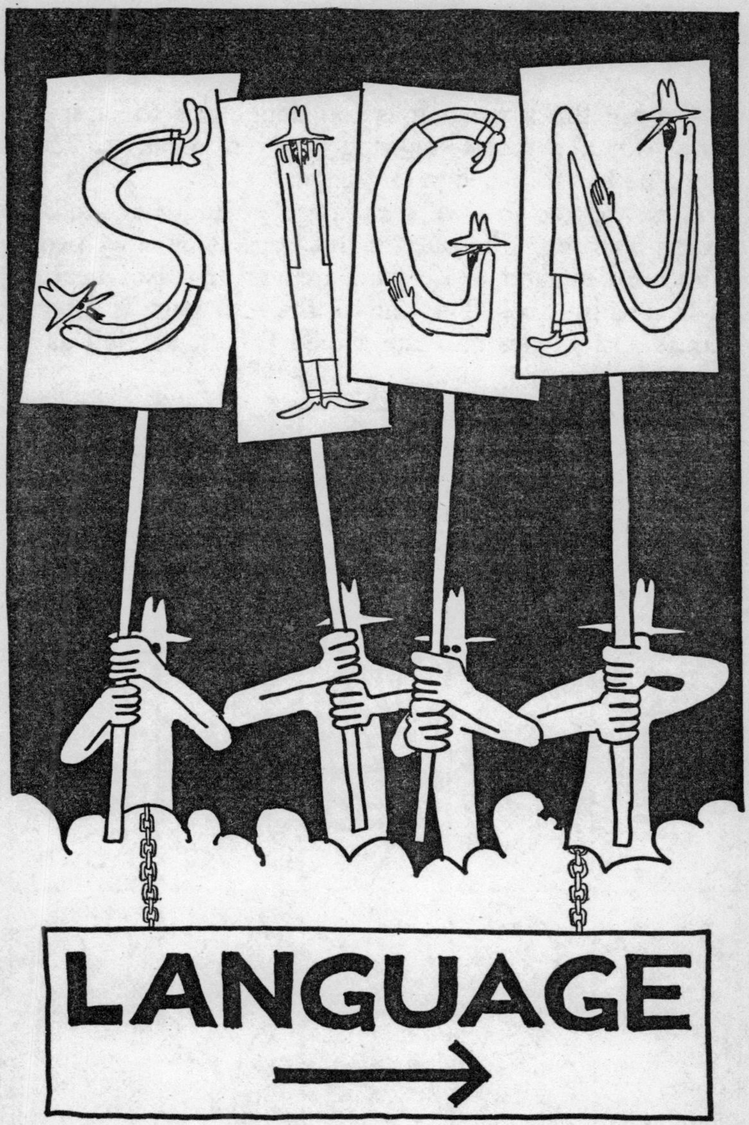
SIGN
LANGUAGE

# SIGN LANGUAGE

There are times when it is too dangerous for a spy to write down a secret message or even speak it. That's when he has to use sign language.

Here are two sorts of sign language and they are both worth learning. The one on this page is used by people who are deaf and those who are very hard of hearing, as well as by spies. The one on the next page is used by scouts and guides and the armed forces, as well as by spies.

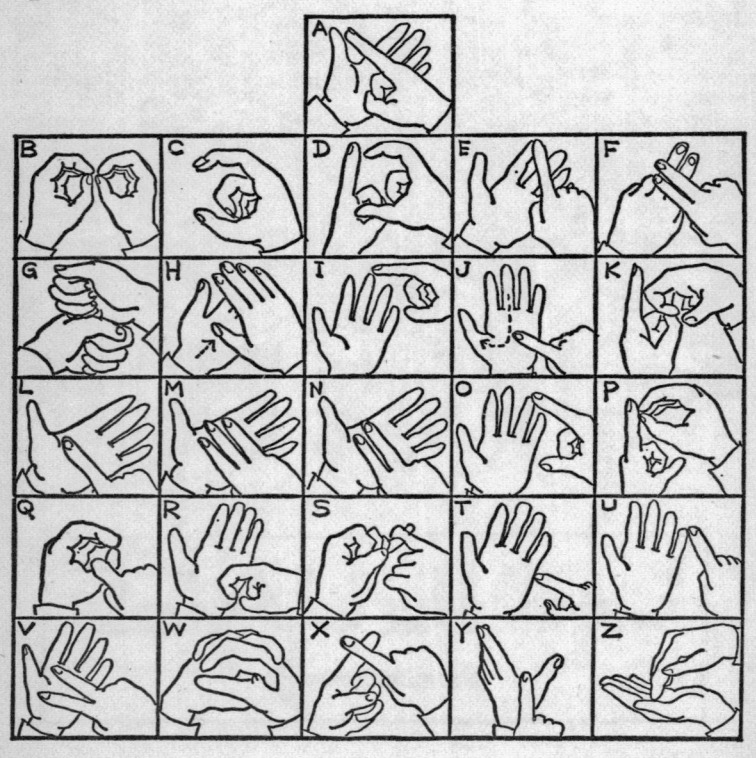

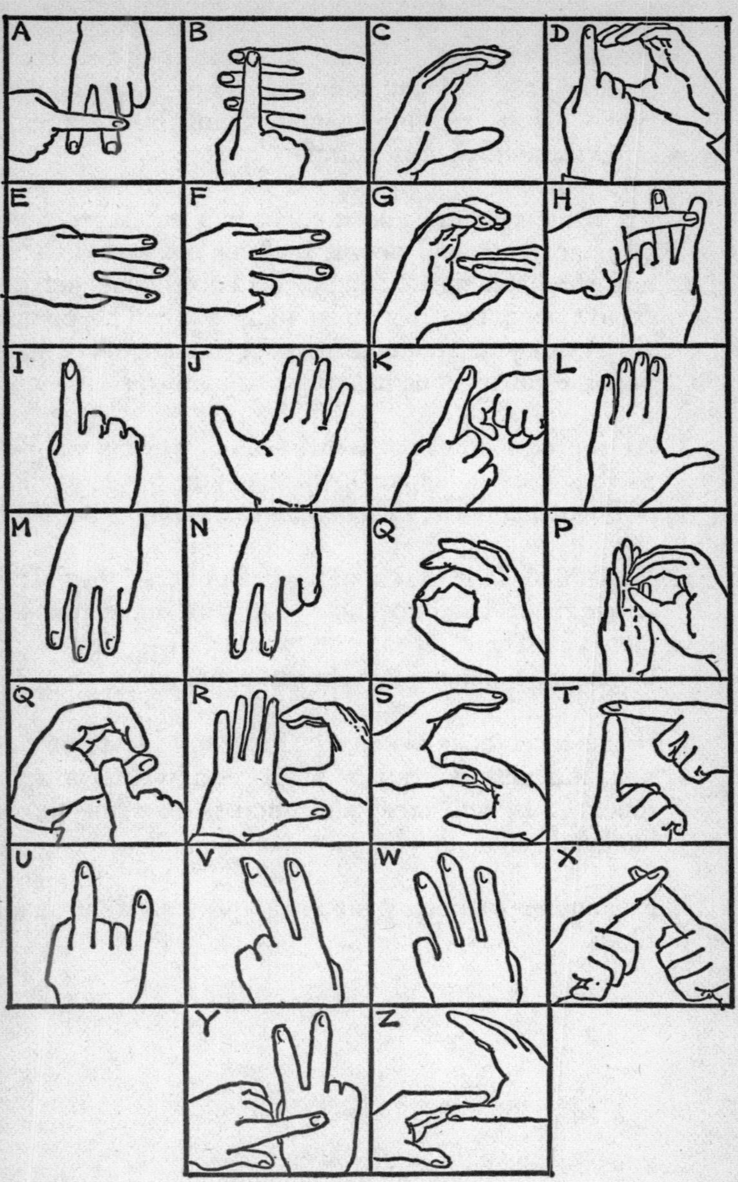
A
B
C
D
E
F
G
H
I
J
K
L
M
N
Q
P
Q
R
S
T
U
V
W
X
Y
Z

Semaphore you know already as a useful cipher. It can also be used as – and was intended to be – a special sign language. When sending secret Semaphore signals, remember these important rules:

1. To show you are about to start a message, wave your arms up and down, making the signal for U and then the signal for N. Wait until you get the 'ready' sign before you actually start. The person to whom you are sending your message will give you the ready sign: it is the Semaphore sign for E.

2. At the end of every word stretch your arms out in the W sign. This shows that you have finished one word and are about to start signalling another.

3. If you make a mistake, cross and uncross your arms above your head to show that you have made a mistake. Then repeat the whole word from the beginning – getting it right this time.

4. If the receiver is not ready for you to start or has not understood your message and wants you to repeat it, he will cross and uncross his arms above his head.

5. Remember to keep your arms quite straight at all times.

123

# BODY SIGNALS

Sometimes you won't be able to use sign language. If you need to tell another spy something very important and very secret and you are both standing in the middle of a crowded room, you can't start telling him in Semaphore! For special emergencies like this, you need Body Signals. Each signal has a different meaning, but no outsider seeing you making the signal would realise that anything unusual was going on. You and your fellow spies should invent your own Body Signals, but to give you the idea, here are some of the signals used by secret agents in the past:

## 1. SCRATCHING YOUR HEAD
Meaning: We are being watched. Don't say or do anything.

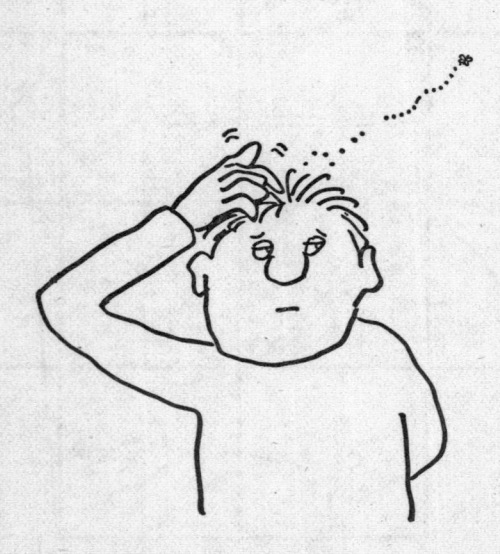

## 2. SCRATCHING RIGHT EAR
**Meaning:** Escape as quickly as possible. The enemy are closing in.

## 3. PULLING LEFT EAR LOBE
**Meaning:** Meet me later at our usual secret meeting place.

## 4. HANDS BEHIND HEAD AND A BIG YAWN
**Meaning:** The Spy Master wants to see you urgently. Report to him at once.

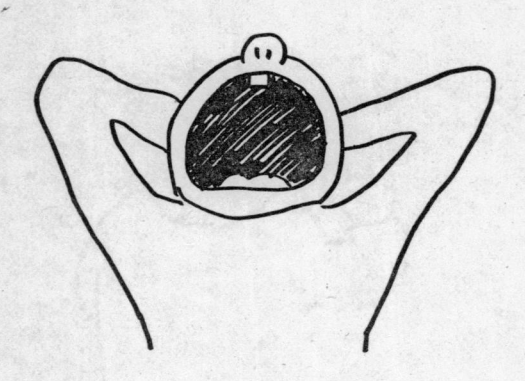

## 5. ARMS FOLDED AND WHISTLING
**Meaning:** I have a message for you which I will leave at the 'dead-letter box' as arranged.

## 6. SNEEZING FIT
**Meaning:** The Spy Ring is meeting for a special secret session at Headquarters tonight. Be there.

## 7. HANDS ON HIPS
**Meaning:** Your cover has been broken. The enemy will get you if you don't leave the country immediately.

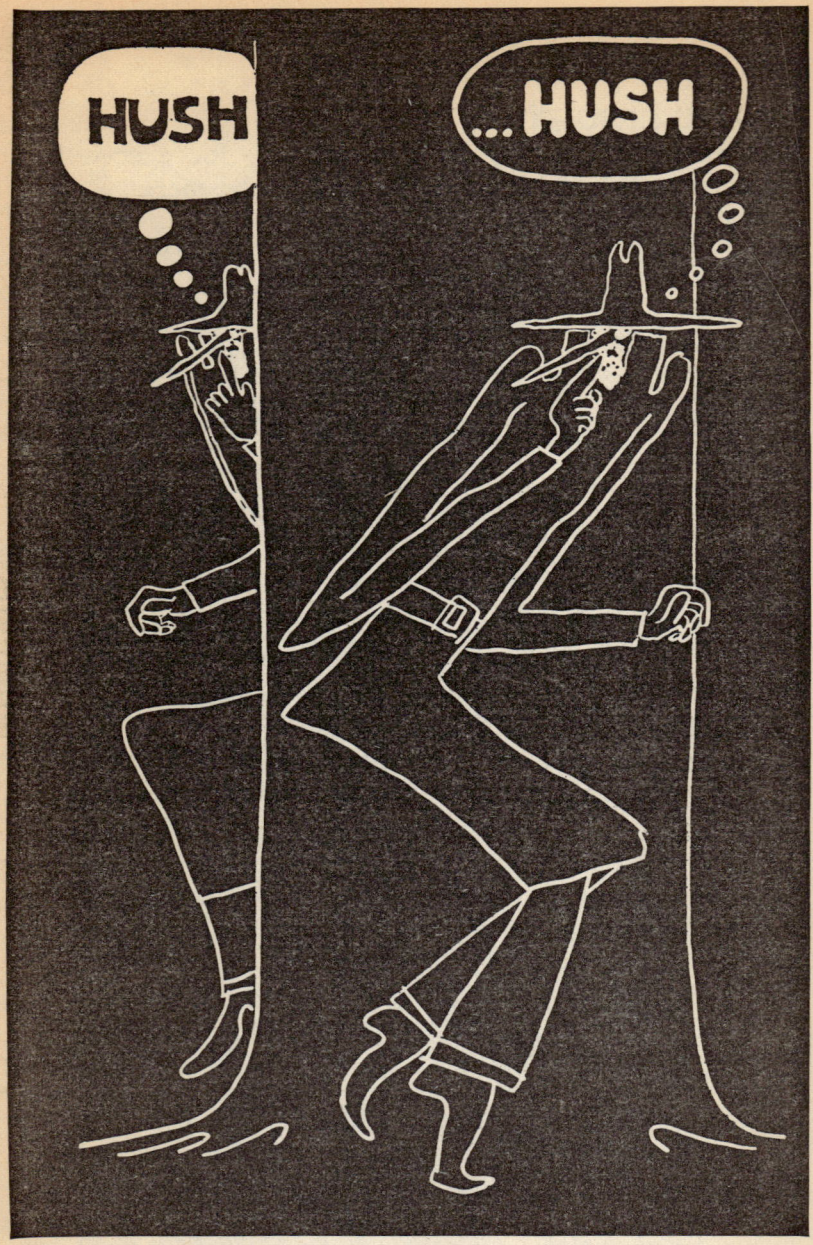

EVERYTHING YOU HAVE READ IN THIS BOOK IS TOP SECRET. REMEMBER TO KEEP IT A SECRET. AND IF THE ENEMY CATCH YOU READING **THE BIG BOOK OF SECRETS** EXPLAIN THAT YOU BOUGHT IT BY MISTAKE: YOU WERE REALLY LOOKING FOR A STORY ABOUT WINNIE THE POOH; GOOD LUCK.